There are millions of ants on our planet.

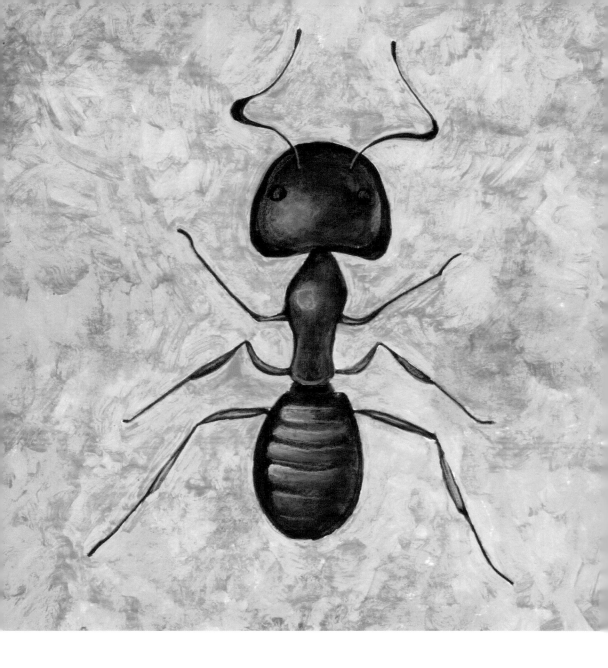

Ants are insects and have six legs.

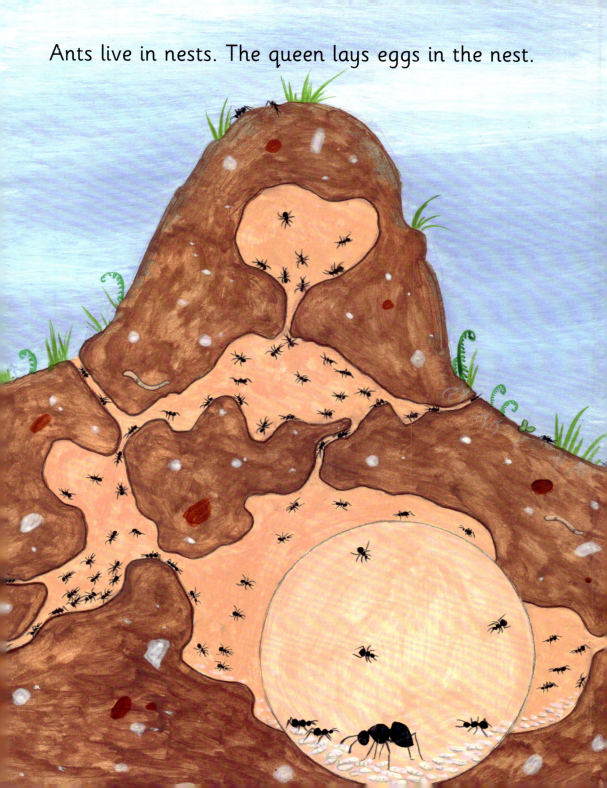
Ants live in nests. The queen lays eggs in the nest.

Worker ants are female. They have long legs and run fast.

Worker ants lack wings, but the queen and male ants have wings.

Worker ants fetch food and bring it to the nest.

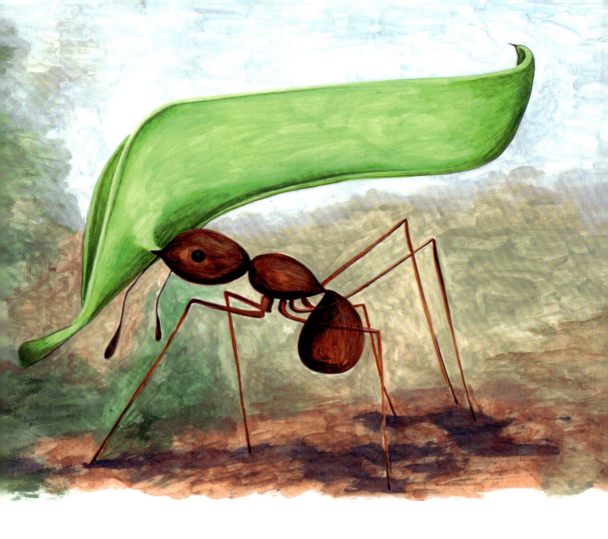

Ants are strong and can lift things that are much bigger than them, such as bits of plants.

When you don't sit still, Mum or Dad will say:
'Have you got ants in your pants?'